Wantagh: A History

D1528237

Wantagh: A History

Emma Alexander

To those who helped me along the way. Thank you.

Contents

Chapter One: The Beginning

The history of Long Island begins with the last Ice Age. During the Pleistocene Epoch, the last ice age spanned from about 2.6 million years ago to about 11,000 years ago and created a series of glacial advances and retreats. During the peak of this ice age, massive sheets of ice covered much of North America.

It is within the Pleistocene Epoch that Long Island was formed. As stated by Robert Villani in his book *Long Island A Natural History*, the island was created when a series of land modifications occurred as a result of glacial retreats. Coincidentally, this Epoch also resulted in the entirety of the island being covered in ice. It is not until 11,000 years ago that a warming climate began to uncover the island underneath (Villani 13). Therefore the island itself has only been in existence for roughly 6,000 to 8,000 years, making Long Island practically infantile, according to Villani (9). In addition to Long Island, this ice age also created Niagara Falls (Scott).

Human beings, on the other hand, were actually in existence before the creation of Long Island. The first humans to enter North America arrived around 11,500 years ago and entered the continent through a now underwater land bridge known as the Bering Land Bridge (Rincon). It is around this time that the first inhabitants of the island existed, even though the island itself was yet to be formed in the shape we know it as today. These first inhabitants were known as Paleo-Americans, with the prefix "paleo" coming from the Greek word *palaios*, meaning "old" or "ancient."

Like most early peoples, the Paleo-Americans were both hunters and gathers. These individuals also fished and were considered semi-nomadic as they moved their homes throughout the seasons in search of food. Long Island would have been a good home for many Paleo-Americans due to the island's geographical features. The soil of the island was incredibly fertile due to the deposits left behind during the last glacial retreat. Moreover, the land's proximity to water would have been incredibly beneficial for individuals who relied on fishing as a means of survival.

Paleo-Americans were the very first inhabitants of Long Island and were the ancestors of the Native American tribes which the Europeans would encounter when they arrived on the island in the early 17th century.

Chapter Two: Native American Tribes Before European Contact

The Native American culture of Long Island, and North America at large, is an incredibly important aspect of history that is of little weight in the modern history textbook. If not for the fact that Native Americans were the ones who saved many European colonies from ruin, there would likely be no remembrance of these vibrant cultures in our history books at all. The cultures of the tribes that inhabited Long Island and Wantagh were incredibly vibrant, and this chapter aims to provide a basis of information on the first peoples of the island.

The first thing one must know about the Native Americans who inhabited the island was that there was not one tribe of individuals, but rather thirteen. In anthropology, the term "tribe" is defined as a type of social organization that contains some aspects of political organization and contains traditions of language, culture, and ideology (Prine Pauls). These thirteen tribes each had their own chief, however, all tribes also acknowledged the authority of an inter-tribal grand sachem, who was responsible for all tribes on the island.

It is unknown what the tribes called themselves, for no written records were kept by the Native peoples. Ethnographic data on Native American culture suggests that the Long Island tribes defined themselves in terms of "lineage and clan membership," although what these terms were has been lost in history (Strong 25). Interestingly, the first list of names for the tribes of Long Island was not a list of thirteen tribes, but rather seven. In the journal of Reverend Charles Wolley, a minister of the church of England who visited the island in 1678, it is written that "there are several Nations which may be more properly called Tribes of Indians." The Reverend then goes on to list seven tribes he had encountered on the island. Wolley listed the following as being the Native Tribes of the island: Rockoway, Sea-qua-ta-eg, Unckah-chau-ge, Se-tauck, Ocqua-baug, Shin-na-cock, which was described as being "the greatest Tribe" and Mun-tauk (Wolley). However, some tribes that Wolley had come in contact with through trade were not mentioned in his list, such as the Matinecocks. The idea of thirteen Native American tribes first came into existence through Silas Wood, a man considered to be Long Island's first historian. Wood, likely unaware of Wolley's journal as there had been very few copies in circulation in North America at the time, wrote in 1824 that he identified thirteen "tribes" that occupied the island (Wood). Wood identified the following tribes: the Matinicoc, the Nissaquague, the Setauket, the Corchaug, the

Canarse, the Rockaway, the Merrikoke, the Marsapeague, the Secatauge, the Patchogue, the Shinecoc, the Manhanset, and the Montauk. (Wood's spellings for the tribes were utilized here). According to John A. Strong, a Professor Emeritus of History and American Studies at Long Island University, "Wood examined the Dutch and English records carefully, but he appears to have relied primarily on the deeds for his conclusions about tribal names and boundaries" (Strong 26). Wood's list became widely circulated and most historical references written after his time state that there were thirteen tribes occupying the island. Because he relied on deeds and not first-hand contact with specific tribes, it is postulated that the actual number of tribes that lived on the island may be more numerous or less so than what Wood described. Therefore, due to disputes amongst historians and the fact that there are no written records of what these Native peoples called themselves, one must take the names and number of tribes that were believed to have occupied the island with a grain of salt.

Regardless of the exact names and number of tribes that lived on the island, in Wantagh, it is believed that both the Merricks and the Marsapeaques lived in the area.

Language

It is likely that both the Merricks and the Marsapeaques spoke either a dialect of Munsee or were the linguistic ancestors of the Unquachog people of the 18th century. The exact dialect of these tribes is unknown as an eastward drift in population beginning in the 17th century made it difficult to determine exactly what language these tribes spoke. However, it is assumed that the tribes did speak similar dialects of an Algonquian language, as the area in which the two tribes resided typically overlapped with one another. There are about thirty Algonquian languages known today, although there are likely many more dialects of the language that were lost due to a lack of written records (Sturtevant). The Munsee language is also closely related to the American Delaware, or Leni Lenape, but is considered to be a distinct language by linguists. The word *Merricks* means "at the barren land" while *Massapequas* means "great water land" ("The Tribes of Long Island").

Homes

Like other Algonquian-speaking tribes, the Merricks and the Marsapeaques both lived in wigwams, which were dome-shaped structures made of a wooden frame and covered with materials that varied by region. On Long Island, the tribes likely used reeds, due to their proximity to water, or animal hides or cloth. Wigwams typically had one to two doors, which had coverings made of animal hide or a woven mat that could be let down for privacy. A fire pit for cooking would be inside, while a hole in the top of the wigwam would help with ventilation and allow the smoke from the firepit to escape. According to David Martine, a historian specializing in Native American history on Long Island, these villages "would have been made up of several of these wigwams placed around a central clearing in which public activities would have taken place such as work, ceremonies or planting gardens" (Martine). Wigwams are often confused with teepees, which were used by Native American tribes out on the Great Plains, although both were able to be dismantled and transported if the need arose.

Religion and Burial Practices

While there are no written records on the specific beliefs of the Merricks or the Marsapeaques, both tribes likely practiced animism. Animism is defined as the belief that spirits reside in all objects in nature. In other words, these tribes believed that everything, from trees to grass to rocks, has a spirit ("Animism"). The spiritual world was believed to be very interconnected with the physical world. Although they did not believe in a divine god or being, these tribes believed in an all-encompassing force known as the Gitche Manitou, which translates to the Great Spirit. Gitche Manitou was believed to be present in all living things as well as non-living things, such as the moon and stars. It is also possible that shamans were also prevalent in the spiritual life of these tribes. Shamans were tribal members who were believed to have a spiritual connection and because of this connection, could protect people from malicious spirits by performing cleansing ceremonies. It was also believed that some shamans could interpret dreams, giving a glimpse into the future, as the Algonquin people believed that dreams could show a person things about the future (Cummins).

In terms of burial practices, one's burial was typically dependent on their standing within the tribe. For example, the chief of each tribe, or people in high social standing, would be cleaned and wrapped and then placed on a wooden scaffold within a communal tomb. For the common tribe member upon death, the body was placed in ossuaries, in this instance being large burial mounds.

Culture

The Merricks and the Marsapeaques were mainly hunters and gatherers, although farming practices were still somewhat present. As these tribes lived along the water, fishing was prevalent. Either spearfishing or trapping the fish was typically utilized. These tribes likely utilized clambakes, which were large open pits in the sand used to cook seafood. The men of the tribe also hunted game such as moose and beaver. The women would gather nuts and berries from nature as well as cultivate crops such as corn and beans. Dead fish were often utilized to fertilize these crops.

All members of the tribes were considered to be equal, and both men and women were expected to perform duties for the betterment of the tribe. While the men took care of hunting, women were in charge of everything having to do with the home. This included collecting firewood, looking after the food storage, and making clothing. Some of the tribes were matriarchal, meaning the women played a central role in governing the community. In terms of family structure, grandparents and elders played an extremely important role in these tribes. These provided both spiritual and governing guidance, helped to relay the stories of their ancestors to new generations and helped to look after the youngest members of the tribe. Elders of the tribe, therefore, were greatly honored and respected.

Chapter 3: European Arrival

In the early 17th century, Henry Hudson, an English explorer, briefly explored the Hudson River in the search for a northwest passage. The northwest passage was greatly sought for at the time, as it would provide a direct route through waterways from the Atlantic to the Pacific. Hudson at the time was sailing on behalf of the Dutch East India Company, a trading company established in 1602 in the present-day Netherlands. While Hudson and his crew eventually turned back as their search for a northwest passage through the Hudson river was fruitless, this laid the foundation for Dutch settlement on Long Island. In addition, this 1609 voyage is also the first time that the Long Island natives came into contact with Europeans ("Henry Hudson"). After this initial contact, Europeans, specifically, the Dutch, began to flock to the area to trade with the natives.

After Hudson's voyage, Hudson went back to his roots and sailed again, this time for his home country of England. The Dutch, however, flocked to the area Hudson explored for opportunities for exploration and trade with the native peoples. One of these individuals was Adriaen Block, a Dutch tradesman, and explorer. Block made numerous voyages to the lower Hudson region to trade with the natives there. Typically, explorers would obtain beaver pelts from the natives in the region, as these were incredibly profitable back in Europe. In a 1613 voyage, Block explored the area now known as the Long Island Sound and is considered to be the first European to do so. After Block concluded his expedition, he drew a map of the area he had explored. The map drawn by Block is considered to be the first map that showcased Long Island as being an actual island as opposed to a peninsula (Yost).

It is around this time that the Dutch began to colonize the western portion of Long Island, as well as the region that is considered to be present-day Manhattan and Staten Island. The Dutch named their new home "Lange Eylant," with Lange meaning long ("Long Island"). These Dutch settlers are considered the first European settlers of the island, and some were likely to have lived in or near Wantagh, due to its proximity to water as well as the island of Manhattan. The Dutch named their settlement New Amsterdam, and thus, the foundation for what would one day become New York City was born. These individuals made their livelihood mainly through the fur trade with the local Native American tribes.

And yet, during the time the Dutch settled the western portion of the island, the English had settled the eastern portion. This caused tension between the two groups as each claimed the island as their own. In 1664, the Dutch surrendered New Amsterdam, present-day Manhattan, and the surrounding area, which included the western portion of the island. The English now owned the entirety of the island ("About Long Island").

Chapter Four: English Colonization

Of course, the English wouldn't want to be hindered in their colonization efforts by something as simple as the Dutch claiming the land for themselves. Therefore before the acquisition of western Long Island by the English in the 1660s, Englishmen from Connecticut explored the Hempstead Plains. This area, still known as the Hempstead Plains today, is located in the center of the Town of Hempstead. Back then, the area would have stretched much larger than it does today, and likely would have covered most of the western portion of the island (Feldmann). The Englishmen believed that this area would be good for farming and cattle grazing and thus wished to settle the land, which included present-day Wantagh.

The English received permission from the Dutch to settle on the Hempstead Plains. The Dutch likely agreed because they were mainly concerned with their colonization further west in Manhattan. Due to this agreement, the first official European settlers came to Wantagh. While there may have been Dutch settlers in Wantagh prior to this time, the English settlers described below are among those for whom there are historical documents to support them living in Wantagh.

The English Settlers

The first European settlers of Wantagh were led by Reverend Richard Denton, a presbyterian minister. Richard Denton was born in Yorkshire England in 1602. He attended Cambridge University in the 1620s and became a priest in 1623. In 1635, he came to the English settlement of Watertown, Massachusetts to preach, before moving to Connecticut in 1641. It is around this time that Reverend Denton, his family, and others decided to move to the Hempstead Plains to try and begin a new life (Seibel). Even though the area was currently owned by the Dutch, they agreed to allow these English settlers to live in the area. These individuals settled in the area that is now present-day Wantagh and Seaford.

Among these first individuals were the Seaman and Jackson families, who settled in the area in 1643. The group from Connecticut purchased the land they settled on from the Mericokes and Marsapeaques who lived in the Wantagh-Seaford area in 1644. The land included in the sale was about 6,000 acres, a significant portion of the

Hempstead Plains. In the same year, Robert Jackson built the first dwelling in Wantagh and many more soon followed.

Sign commemorating the original site of the first building of Jerusalem: the home of Robert Jackson.

The patriarch of the Jackson family at the time was Robert Jackson. Born in England around 1615, Jackson and his father were both Separatists, meaning they wished to separate themselves from the Church of England. In 1640, Jackson and his father traveled to Massachusetts along with Reverend Denton to search for religious freedom. Jackson followed Reverend Denton once again in 1644 and finally settled on the Hempstead Plains. John Seaman, the patriarch of the Seaman family, was also an English Protestant, born in Essex, England (Toscano). Like the Jackson family, the Seaman family also traveled to the Hempstead Plains in search of religious freedom. Both the Jackson and the Seaman families would be essential in the establishment of a town known as Jerusalem, which would one day become Wantagh (Manton).

The Seaman and Jackson families were a part of a larger wave of English Protestants searching for religious freedom in North America. Many of these individuals were Quakers, also known as the Religious Society of Friends. Quakers believed that everyone had Christ within them, a stark contrast to the ideology of one performing ceremonies and rituals to become closer to God. Moreover, Quakers believed that women and men were spiritual equals, a radical idea at the time ("Quakers"). The Religious Society of Friends was essential in establishing the settlement of Jerusalem, and remnants of this can still be seen in Wantagh today, with the Quaker Meeting House and cemetery, established in the 1800s, located on Wantagh Avenue.

Others came to Wantagh for farming opportunities, as the Hempstead Plains was a vast, flat and fertile area that allowed for individuals to easily grow crops and raise cattle. For many years after the first settlers arrived, the area would be considered a small community that mainly relied on farming.

Colonial Government

Colonial life in present-day Wantagh was mainly focused on farming and the few influential families that lived in the area. Other than the Jacksons and the Seamans, the Birdsall family was another prominent family that also settled in the area. In 1665, the Duke's Law Convention was held in Hempstead, New York, on March 1. Each English town on the island, of which there were sixteen at the time including in Westchester County, sent two representatives to the convention. One of the representatives for the Wantagh area was Robert Jackson. At the convention, a legal system was established based on the English legal system at the time. This legal system was in use until it was repealed in 1683. The system established a court that would hear the appeals from the decisions of town courts ("Hempstead Convention of 1665"). By being chosen to represent the area now known as Wantagh at this convention, Jackson became a founding father of Hempstead.

In 1666, the settlers were given a charter for the area, which they named Jerusalem, meaning "city of peace." The charter included what is today northern Wantagh as well as southern Levittown. The name Jerusalem was influenced by the Quakers who settled in the area, who likely viewed the land as a place where they could practice their religion in peace ("Wantagh Local History").

Sign commemorating the original settlement of Jerusalem, officially established in 1644.

The local government of Jerusalem was mainly set up in the English style of governance of town meetings. Town meetings are considered to be the most direct form of democracy, as in early colonial Jerusalem, community members would vote directly on issues. Leaders of the town, such as magistrates, were elected during these town meetings. Because there was no jail in the area at the time, punishment for crimes included public whippings, fines, time in the stocks, and, for severe crimes, death. These punishments would be administered by elected town officials. As the population grew, the government of the community shifted away from the popular vote and more towards a representative government (McKernan and Gordon).

Colonial Life

The center of the community was located along present-day Wantagh Avenue, which at the time was known as Jerusalem Lane. Today, many historical sites can be found along Wantagh Avenue, including the site of the original Robert Jackson Homestead and the Wantagh Museum. The community, while mainly composed of farms, also contained a grist mill and sawmill, which were both essential to colonial life.

The road where the grist mill was located is now known as Old Mill Road, where a historical marker designating the spot can still be seen today. Around 1704 the Jackson family was given full mill rights along the Jerusalem River. However, the grist and sawmills were not as essential as farming was to Jerusalem's economy. Early Jerusalem residents, like many colonists on Long Island at the time, relied mainly on farming to get by. Farming was incredibly profitable in the area due to the large amount of fertile land that was perfect for growing crops as well as raising cattle.

The original Grist Mill Building was located on Old Mill Road. The structure would have been used to grind down grains into flour and was incredibly important to colonial life (Courtesy of NY Heritage and the Wantagh Preservation Society).

In colonial Jerusalem, women were in charge of taking care of the household. Typical duties included cleaning, sewing, and educating the children. Men, on the other hand, looked after their land and were in charge of governing the town. Children spent their time in different ways based on their gender. Boys were typically taught how to farm and trade while girls were taught how to take care of the home. Both girls and boys were taught how to read, typically so they could read religious texts ("National Geographic Society"). In terms of religious life, women likely had more of a say than in other colonies in the United States at the time, as Jerusalem was made up mainly of Quakers. Families partook in local festivities typically having to do with farming and cattle. Activities such as horse racing were also common at the time.

Other Individuals in Jerusalem

A lack of significant conflicts with local tribes indicates that the settlers of Jerusalem got along fairly well with the neighboring tribes, even though conflicts in larger areas, such as New York City, were common. Trade was likely prominent between the English and the Natives. It is important to note that as the town of

Jerusalem, and neighboring towns grew, the local Native population began to decline greatly. Many Natives were forced to leave their ancestral lands to make room for the increasing number of English settlers who claimed the land their family had lived on for generations. Other than the names of several towns on Long Island, a significant impact of the Native peoples of the island in present-day Wantagh is the way the roads are laid out. The original English colonists in the area used Native trade and transportation routes, and over time these roads became increasingly popular and were eventually paved. Therefore, while no physical structures from the native peoples remain, the way the town is set up can in part be attributed to the natives who lived in the area for hundreds of years (McKernan and Gordon). In addition, two Native American reservations remain on Long Island today, the Shinnecock Reservation and the Poospatuck Reservation, both of which are located in Suffolk County.

Additionally, slavery in Jerusalem was also prevalent due to the large amount of farming done in the area. However since the area was not as warm as in the southern colonies, huge plantations with hundreds of enslaved individuals were not typical in the area. Enslaved individuals were first brought to the island in the 1650s. A typical Jerusalem family might own two of these people, although those on larger farms would have owned more. Some members of both the Jackson and Seaman families owned enslaved individuals that worked on their family farms.

Up until the American Revolution, New York, and therefore Jerusalem by extension, had some of the strictest slavery laws in colonial America. Slavery was illegal when the Dutch occupied the area but with the arrival of the English so too came the legalization of slavery. The 1702 Act of the Regulation of Slaves prohibited trade with any enslaved person without their master's consent. A slave rebellion in New York City in 1712 resulted in the passing of much harsher slave codes. Slave codes were any rules that were based on the concept that enslaved individuals were property, not human beings.

The Slave Rebellion of 1712 began at night on April 6, 1712, in Manhatten. After a fire was set to an outhouse, the signal to begin the revolt, those in bondage began to fire into the crowd of white people that had gathered outside their homes to see the commotion. This resulted in the deaths of nine white colonists, and, while some were pardoned, a brutal execution for the enslaved individuals found guilty for the rebellion. Amongst those found guilty, manners of execution included being burned alive, starved, and crushed by a wheel. This event led to harsh slavery laws, including slaveholders being able to punish their slaves however they saw fit, enslaved individuals being unable to congregate in large groups (typically more than three people), and those in bondage being prohibited from owning a firearm ("New York Slave Rebellion of 1712").

Thus while slavery wasn't hugely prevalent in Jerusalem at the time, those in bondage that did reside in the area had the possibility of being treated horribly. While records indicate that the Jacksons and Seamans treated the enslaved people they owned fairly well, it is of importance to note that these individuals were not in the area of their own free will. They were forced to reside here. Yet while slavery did play a role in establishing the town of Jerusalem, attitudes in Jerusalem towards slavery would shift after the American Revolution.

Chapter Five: The American Revolution

The American Revolutionary War forever altered both the town lines and the beliefs of the residents of Hempstead, of which the town of Jerusalem was a part of. Prior to the American Revolution, which began in 1775, Hempstead and North Hempstead were one town. However, residents of the town staunchly disagreed on which side of the revolution was to be supported. Those residing in the northern section of the town were mainly Patriots, believing the thirteen colonies should break away from English rule. Those resigning on the south shore, however, were loyal to the King and therefore were aptly named Loyalists. This difference in opinion would eventually lead to the town being divided into North and South Hempstead, with Jerusalem being a part of South Hempstead, in 1784. Jerusalem sat on the southern shore of the island and therefore many of the residents were Loyalists (McKernan and Gordon).

And yet not all Jerusalem residents were Loyalists. Numerous residents within the community, including some who were descendants of the original settlers of Jerusalem, were devoted Patriots. Some of these individuals include members of the Jackson, Seaman, and Birdsall families.

Overview of the American Revolution

The tension leading up to the American Revolution began when the British ended the period of salutary neglect that they had practiced in the 17th and 18th centuries. The period of salutary neglect allowed for the thirteen colonies to more or less govern themselves with very little intervention from the British government. Following the end of the French and Indian War, also known as the Seven Years' War, in 1763, Great Britain was in a massive amount of debt. Because of this debt, the British began to heavily tax their colonies in North America, which stretched from what is now Georgia all the way north to New Hampshire. Great Britain began to heavily tax the colonists without them having any say in the manner, which greatly angered the colonists. This is where the phrase "No taxation without representation" comes from, which is attributed to James Otis, a lawyer from Massachusetts, who said that "taxation without representation is tyranny" ("On This Day"). This lack of representation ultimately led to rising tension that began the American Revolutionary War.

The war officially began at the battles of Lexington and Concord on April 19, 1775, when the colonial militia, nicknamed the minutemen, attacked after a shot was fired in a standoff with the British. While it is unknown which side ultimately fired first, this "shot heard 'round the world" officially started the American Revolution ("Overview of the American Revolutionary War"). From this point forward, the war would be between the Continental Army, the name for the colonist's army made up of a group of untrained men led by George Washington, and the British Army, a military powerhouse.

While many significant battles occurred during the American Revolution, the one that was closest to Jerusalem residents was the Battle of Long Island. The battle, also known as the Battle of Brooklyn, was the first major battle after the colonists declared their independence on July 4th, 1776. The battle began on August 27, 1776, and lasted two days. The British attacked and surrounded Continental Army forces in Manhattan and Long Island to cut off New England from the rest of the colonies. The British army forced Washington to retreat, which resulted in the British capturing New York City and Long Island. Washington's quick thinking allowed for the army to escape, regroup and continue to fight against the British ("Battle of Long Island"). After the retreat of the Continental Army at the Battle of Long Island, the island was occupied by Hessian soldiers, German soldiers hired by the British to fight in the American Revolution. While Jerusalem was mainly loyal to the king, the Hessian soldiers who occupied Jerusalem during the war were largely despised by residents due to their harsh disposition and their constantly raiding farms for supplies.

The American Revolutionary War ended with the Battle of Yorktown on October 19th, 1781 in Virginia. The war officially ended in 1783 when Great Britain formally recognized the United States as being an independent nation in the 1783 Treaty of Paris. While most of the fighting wasn't done near the island, many from Jerusalem were heavily involved in the revolution. On both sides of the war, Jerusalem residents fought for their beliefs. Some of their stories are discussed below.

Prominent Jerusalem Citizens of the Revolution

Captain Richard Jackson, a descendant of the Jackson family that settled Jerusalem, was a Patriot during the American Revolution. Jackson commanded the Jerusalem Company of the Queens County Militia during the war. Jackson was also the father of Jane Jackson, whose love story with a Hessian soldier is well known in Wantagh today. According to legend, Jane fell in love with a Hessian soldier named John Althause. As the legend goes, Jane snuck out of her house, which can still be seen today on Wantagh Avenue, while the help of a slave, who then carried her on his back through the marshes to the field where the high school sits today. It is there that Jane and John met to escape Jerusalem and elope in secret. While records indicate this story has largely been fabricated over time, as there are few records to indicate the validity of the story, Jane and Althause were in a relationship that Jane's family didn't approve of, and the two would go on to be married and have children. The two are buried at the Jackson Cemetery on Wantagh Avenue (Pfeiffer).

The home on Wantagh Avenue where Captain Richard Jackson and his family, including daughter Jane Jackson, once lived.

The Jackson Cemetery on Wantagh Avenue next to St. Francis de Chantel Church. Many members of prominent Wantagh families are buried here including members of the Jackson and Althause families. Jane Jackson and her husband are also buried here.

Lt. Zebulum Seaman was a Patriot and a lieutenant with the Jerusalem militia when the Revolutionary War began. The Jerusalem militia would have been comprised of regular citizens of Jerusalem with little to no military training. These individuals would have been mainly farmers, as farming was the main source of income in Jerusalem at the time, as well as shopkeepers and merchants. There were around one hundred men in the Jerusalem militia. Seaman joined the Continental Army when the Revolutionary War began. He died in 1784 in his 60s ("Long Island Surnames").

Benjamin Jackson, another Patriot, is said to have led sea patrols along the coast of Long Island. These patrols were done to prevent Loyalists from providing British troops with supplies. Jackson was responsible for about eight miles along the South Bay, and he is credited with capturing about one hundred small boats. Additionally, it is said that he hid local cattle from the British army. He is buried at the Jackson Cemetery on Wantagh Avenue (McKernan and Gordon).

Benjamin Birdsall was born in 1776 and was a Lieutenant in the Continental Army during the American Revolutionary War. He was also a member of the Assembly, the provisional government set up by the colonists during the American Revolution, from 1777 to 1783. During the war, he was captured by the British. It is at this time that he was bestowed the rank of Colonel. Prior to the war, he had married Freelove Jones in 1763 and after the war, the two, along with their children, settled into a house that they bought in 1779 on Old Mill Road. Birdsall was a successful farmer and owned the gristmill across the street from his home. Birdsall died in 1798 and was remembered as being a man who worked hard to fix his farm after the war. The house on Old Mill Road still stands to this day, and one can see a plaque commemorating Birdsall outside it (O'Connor-Arena).

Photograph of the Grist Mill and Birdsall-Mill House looking South on Old Mill Road. (Courtesy of NY Heritage and the Wantagh Preservation Society).

Photograph of the Birdsall-Mill House today. The Grist Mill building has been demolished.

Not all in Jerusalem found success during the Revolutionary War, such as the case with Parmenus Jackson. Jackson, the uncle of General Jacob Jackson who fought in the Continental Army, was a wealthy Jerusalem farmer who was well-respected within the community. On January 19, 1776, Parmenus, along with other members of the Jackson family and residents of Jerusalem, signed a Declaration of Association. This meant that those who signed would remain neutral in the war with Britain. In 1781, Jackson was beaten by British soldiers, who were looking for Jackson's money, and later died due to his wounds. At the time of his death, Jackson was married to Elizabeth Birdsall. In his will, Jackson left his assets to Elizabeth as well as their four children; they had two daughters and two sons ("Parmenus Jackson Sr.").

Chapter Six: The Early 19th Century

After the Revolutionary War ended in 1783, the town of Jerusalem was now officially a part of the newly independent United States of America. And yet, life in Jerusalem was very similar to what it was before the war. Up until the War of 1812, community life was quiet and there was little change in the community. Jerusalem was still a farming community at heart, and many relied on their farms to sustain their way of living. However, the war had brought about changes, and one such change was individuals' attitudes towards slavery.

<u>Slavery After the American Revolution</u>

While in many cases, slave codes remained just as harsh as ever, the American Revolution did bring forth ideas of freedom and liberty into the minds of many. Therefore attitudes towards slavery shifted and some who had previously owned slaves were now faced with a moral dilemma. Thomas Jackson was one of these individuals. Jackson was a war veteran from the American Revolution who fought in the Battle of Long Island and was a member of the prominent Jackson family. At some point near the end of the war, Jackson's family freed the enslaved individuals they had owned, which included Jeffrey Jackson and his wife Kate, as well as other Black individuals. Jeffery, now a free man, bought twenty acres of land from Thomas Jackson in 1808 (Watson). It is on this land that Jeffery Jackson and other newly-freed people created a community where they farmed their own crops and lived. This area was nicknamed "The Brush."

Today, there are two burial grounds located where the Brush would have been, the Old Burying Ground on Oakfield Avenue, and the Harold Avenue Cemetery, located on private property on Harold Avenue ("Harold Avenue Cemetery"). Jeffrey Jackson was buried at the Harold Avenue Cemetery, which was a part of the land that he bought from Thomas Jackson. Jeffrey Jackson's descendants lived on the land he bought for generations.

It is important to note that while some became abolitionists after the American Revolution, the Quakers who resided in Jerusalem were always anti-slavery. This made it much safer for freed Black men and women to live in the area after they were released from bondage. The community they formed, "The Brush," would have been located in western Wantagh and would have stretched into present-day Bellmore. After the

American Revolution, slavery was virtually nonexistent in Jerusalem and both Black and white individuals lived and worked side-by-side, even though there was a segregation of different races.

On July 4, 1827, slavery officially ended in New York State. Prior to 1827, New York had passed a Gradual Emancipation Act in 1799 which freed the children of enslaved individuals but forced them into indentured servitude until they became adults ("When Did Slavery End in New York State?"). 1827 marked the official end to slavery in New York State, although in New York City the illegal international slave trade was still incredibly profitable to those involved (Diouf). Yet in Jerusalem, and Long Island as a whole, this was not prevalent and the now free individuals formed communities of their own and made a living for themselves.

The War of 1812

The War of 1812 was the first major conflict that disrupted the peaceful farming community of Jerusalem after the American Revolution. Many from Jerusalem fought in the war, including US Army Brigadier General Jacob Seaman Jackson, who is buried at the Jackson Cemetery. The War of 1812 once again was a conflict between the United States and Great Britain, this time over the impressment of U.S. soldiers and trade restrictions. While the United States suffered greatly, with the nation's capital in Washington D.C. being burned to the ground, the U.S. ultimately won the war. The war officially ended with the Treaty of Ghent on February 17, 1815 ("War of 1812").

First Half of the 19th Century

Farming and raising cattle continued to be the chief means of earning a living in Jerusalem. Some in southern Wantagh also took up fishing and boating as a source of income, due to their proximity to the water. Whaling, which was much more popular in nearby Seaford, was also sometimes done in Jerusalem. The population of Jerusalem also continued to expand at this time.

In 1827, the Quaker Meeting House off of Wantagh Avenue was built. Before 1827, Quakers, or the Religious Society of Friends, met in secret in private homes, barns, and cellars due to religious persecution. A meeting of Quakers in Jericho led to the construction of an official meeting house in the early 19th century. The house was built on farmland and was constructed using oak wood with a stone foundation. It is considered to be the oldest religious structure in Wantagh. A carriage house at the back of the building protected both the carriages and horses from the elements whilst religious services were going on.

The Quaker Meeting House built circa 1827 (Courtesy of NY Heritage and the Wantagh Preservation Society).

Gatherings at the house continued regularly until 1908, and summer meetings continued until 1949. A plaque designating the house as a historical site from 1971 can be seen on the outside wall (Wiebel).

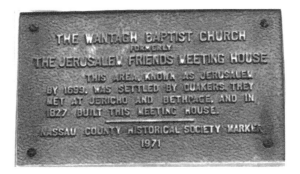

The plaque designating the Jerusalem Friends Meeting House, also known as the Quaker Meeting House, as a historical landmark.

The cemetery next to the meeting house, known as "the Quaker Cemetery," was added to the property in 1861. Originally, the cemetery belonged to the Seaman family. Many important Wantagh residents were buried at the cemetery including numerous Civil War Veterans. The Quaker Cemetery, between Twin Lane North and Twin Lane South, is one of the few Wantagh cemeteries currently open to the public.

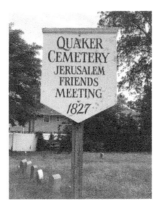

Sign located at the Quaker Cemetery in Wantagh.

The most notable advancement in the history of Jerusalem in the 19th century, however, was not the construction of the Quaker meeting house.

It was the construction of the railroad.

Chapter Seven: The Railroad

While the Long Island Rail Road Company (LIRR) officially began in 1834, it is not the LIRR that first brought the railroad to Jerusalem. Instead, it was the South Side Railroad Company that brought the railroad to Jerusalem many years later in 1867. The South Side Railroad Company was specifically established to be a competitor to the Long Island Rail Road Company. In the late 1800s, the LIRR acquired the Jerusalem branch of the railroad after the South Side Railroad Company formally merged with the LIRR.

The depot itself was known as the Ridgewood Railroad Station. The station was named this because it bordered Brooklyn's Ridgewood Aqueduct, also known as the Brooklyn Water Works. An aquifer located under Long Island was used to supply Brooklyn with much-needed water. Water was pumped through pipes under what is today Sunrise Highway to an aqueduct, located where the Aqueduct Raceway in Queens is today. It was then pumped through an above-ground conduit and directly into Brooklyn.

Construction of the Brooklyn Water Works. The Ridgewood Station can be seen in the background (Courtesy of NY Heritage and the Wantagh Preservation Society).

Yet the aquifer under Long Island also provided island residents themselves with water, and soon enough, the aquifer was not enough to also supply Brooklyn's population with water. Therefore, because of its need for the city's water supply, Brooklyn became a part of New York City in 1898 and the Ridgewood Aqueduct became dormant.

In addition to the depot being known as the Ridgewood Railroad Station, the town of Jerusalem itself was called Ridgewood for a few years beginning in the 1880s. The United States Post Office wouldn't approve the name, however, as another area in New York was also named Ridgewood, located in then-Western Queens County, now Nassau County. Thus, the town needed a new name. Residents pushed to name the area Wantagh to honor a Native American sachem, or grand chief, from the 1640s. From 1891 forward, the town was officially known as Wantagh. This name change meant that Wantagh has had three names throughout its history: Jerusalem, Ridgewood, and finally, Wantagh.

The original depot, constructed in October of 1867, was reconstructed in 1885. The new building was a Victorian-style wooden building "with canopies and sawtooth trim," according to David Morrison, author of "Long Island Railroad: Babylon Branch" (Morrison 53). The walls of the station would have been covered in advertisements. The station also contained a chimney for the potbelly stove inside the station. The stove would have been used to keep station attendants warm during the winter months. The original station stove can still be seen today at the Wantagh Museum.

The original Ridgewood station was constructed in 1867 (Courtesy of NY Heritage and the Wantagh Preservation Society).

View of a train leaving the Wantagh Station. The house on the far right was also a barber shop and bicycle repair shop owned by Wallace Verity(Courtesy of NY Heritage and the Wantagh Preservation Society).

Throughout its long operational history, the original Wantagh station was the place of work for many hardworking Wantagh residents. One of these residents was Emma Whitmore. Born in 1853, Whitmore was a Long Island Railroad station agent from 1890 to 1916 and was one of the first female LIRR station agents. She would have been responsible for the day-to-day operations of the station, including selling tickets, handling baggage, and giving orders to those working on the trains. In addition to her job as a station agent, Whitmore also served as a telegraph operator. She was exceptionally good at her job ("Whitmore, Emma, Wantagh Station Agent").

Emma Whitmore
(Courtesy of NY Heritage and the Wantagh Preservation Society)

Another Wantagh station agent of note is Elvin Bodley. Bodley worked at the station as a ticket agent from 1917 to early 1918. He then "enlisted in the Naval Reserve and served as a wireless operator" in World War I, according to the Wantagh Preservation Society. After the war, he returned to Wantagh to resume his position as a ticket agent. By 1919, he had moved to Massapequa and continued to work as a station agent there ("Elvin Bodley, Wantagh Station Agent").

Elvin Bodley
(Courtesy of NY Heritage and the Wantagh Preservation Society)

The original station remained central to Wantagh's way of life for many years. The station contained an indoor waiting area and an office for ticket agents. As the town expanded, hotels and stores began to spring up around the station. A baggage storage room was added to the station around 1900 and in the 1930s restrooms were added to the station ("1885 Wantagh Station"). The next major change to occur to the Wantagh railroad would be the raising of the tracks in the 1960s, which will be discussed later in this book.

Chapter Eight: The Early 20th Century

Moving into the 20th century, the arrival of the railroad allowed for an increase in trade with residents of New York City for the goods provided by Wantagh farmers, such as milk. The Wells family, for example, owned a large farm in Wantagh.

The farm of Theodore Wells was located on the northwest corner of Wantagh Avenue and Merrick Road (Courtesy of NY Heritage and the Wantagh Preservation Society).

Theodore J. Wells was born in 1852 in Brooklyn. In 1878, he married Phebe Wilmarth. Phebe Wilmarth, born in 1852, was the daughter of another farmer, Alfred Wilmarth. She passed away on July 20, 1921 ("Phebe Wilmarth Wells"). The two lived on Wells's farm in Wantagh and had three children, Mary, Ella, and Leroy. Wells, in addition to being a farmer, was also an active member of the Bellmore Methodist Episcopal Church and served as treasurer and superintendent of the Sunday School there. He died in 1937 ("Theodore J. Wells").

Theodore J. Wells
(Courtesy of NY Heritage and the Wantagh
Preservation Society)

Phebe Wilmarth Wells
(Courtesy of NY Heritage and the Wantagh
Preservation Society)

Life in Wantagh remained centered around farming. But after the construction of the railroad, the town continued to expand and many new buildings were erected.

<u>Wantagh Memorial Congregational Church</u>

One of these buildings was the Wantagh Memorial Congregational Church, built in the 1880s. While this building was torn down in 1964, it served as the only active church in Wantagh for many years. Originally, the church was built by Asa W. Parker, a Brooklyn lawyer. Parker had a summer home in the area and had built and furnished the church as a memorial to his late father. The church was officially dedicated in July of 1888 ("Wantagh Memorial Congregational Church"). The Wantagh Memorial Congregational Church continues to serve Wantagh residents to this day.

The original Wantagh Memorial Congregational Church was built by Asa W. Parker
(Courtesy of NY Heritage and the Wantagh Preservation Society).

This building replaced the original church building that was torn down in 1964. This photo was taken in 1959, while construction on this building was occurring. The church continues to serve Wantagh residents to this day (Courtesy of NY Heritage and the Wantagh Preservation Society).

The Firehouse

Before the construction of the firehouse and company, Wantagh residents discussed the construction of one, but no actions were taken as there was no pressing need for one. After all, Wantagh was a small farming community and fires were few and far between. However, a factory fire in the area changed this. In 1899 William Wilson's bird feather factory, which supplied milliners, or those who made women's hats, with feathers, burned down. This heightened conversation surrounding the construction of a fire company for local residents. In December of 1899, a town meeting was called and unanimously decided to organize the Wantagh Hook, Ladder, and Engine Company. According to the Wantagh Preservation Society, "the first men elected to run the company were Benjamin Carpenter as foreman, D.H. Seymour as assistant, second assistant Frank Seaman, secretary J.T. Seymour, treasurer Alfred Jones and Fred Smith as sergeant at arms" ("Wantagh Fire Department"). The first truck, or horse-drawn wagon, was purchased at the turn of the century and was bought by funds raised by a committee.

The first truck bought for the Wantagh Fire Department in 1901 (Courtesy of NY Heritage and the Wantagh Preservation Society).

Construction of the original Wantagh firehouse began in December of 1902. It was built on a plot of land purchased from Dr. William Rhame located opposite the land that would eventually house the Wantagh hotel. Located south of the railroad tracks, a local carpenter, John Box, was tasked with building the firehouse, then known as the "truck house." He was given $1,275 in his contract to complete the building. The firehouse was to be used by the Wantagh Hook & Ladder Co. No. 1 ("Wantagh Fire Station No. 1, 1910"). The original Wantagh firehouse building is still standing today and is now the Wantagh Autobody Shop.

The Wantagh Hook and Ladder Company in front of the firehouse off of Railroad Avenue in 1910. The young boy in white is Lyman Fussell, the department mascot (Courtesy of NY Heritage and the Wantagh Preservation Society).

The original Wantagh Firehouse building (Courtesy of NY Heritage and the Wantagh Preservation Society).

The Wantagh Autobody Shop, originally the Wantagh Firehouse. The original bell tower is visible in this photograph.

In 1910 the town's blacksmith, George Box, built yet another horse-drawn wagon, or truck. This truck, however, had a Fairbanks gasoline pump added to the back that could pump sixty-six gallons of water in a minute. Prior to this, the fire station utilized individual pails of water to put out fires. In 1914 when WWI began, the upstairs firehouse hall was used as a "reading and writing room for the soldiers and pilots at nearby Lufberry airfield"("Wantagh Fire Department"). The Wantagh fire district was created in 1922, and today, the fire department has five firehouses and a fireboat.

<u>The Post Office</u>

The first location of the Wantagh post office was inside of a general store located at the intersection of Wantagh and Railroad Avenues near the Long Island Railroad. In 1907, due to increasing business, a separate building next to the store was built to serve as the town's post office. The general store at this time was owned by brothers Jonathan and David Fussell. The Fussell brothers were active members of the Wantagh community. They ran the Clifton Farm Boarding Stables in Wantagh in 1891 ("Fussell Brothers…"). According to the Wantagh Preservation, Jonathan Fussell served as postmaster from 1899 to 1913 ("Fussell's General Store…").

The Fussell General Store and the first post office of Wantagh (building on left)
(Courtesy of NY Heritage and the Wantagh Preservation Society).

This building served as the Wantagh post until the mid-1920s. After the post office moved out of the building, and to its present location on Park Avenue, the original post office building was used for a multitude of different things. First, the building was used by Wantagh resident Thomas McGee to run his real estate and insurance agency.

After McGee left the building in 1947, the building served as a taxi stand before briefly housing the Wantagh Republican headquarters in 1976. Soon after, the building was used as a pickle store called Pickle Packin' Momma's. The store, owned by Arlene Weisburd and her daughter Sherri Ginsburg, sold green tomatoes, red peppers, vegetable salad, and chickpea salad in addition to pickles. While the pickles weren't made in the shop, they were brought in from around the island and Manhattan, the pickles were well-received in the community and were described as "excellent" by New York Times reporter Florence Fabricant (Fabricant).

The building was then used for another store, this time one that sold food and tobacco, before Mulcahy's utilized the building as a coat room for their customers until the 1990s. In 1995, Mulcahy's decided to renovate their building and donated the original 1907 post office to the Wantagh Preservation Society. The building was moved to its current home at the Wantagh Museum, this same year. It was renovated to resemble its original appearance and was given a new concrete foundation (*The Information Window*).

The original Wantagh post office building at its current location at the Wantagh Museum.

The current post office is located on Park Avenue across the street from the Wantagh
Public Library.

The Wantagh Hotel

The Wantagh Hotel, built in the early 1900s was a Wantagh staple for decades.
Located on Wantagh Avenue the hotel was originally owned by Bernard Jonas. In 1906,
the hotel was purchased by Plainedge native Henry Ultsch, who made numerous
changes to the hotel. Ultsch held a dance in honor of the reopening of the hotel in May
of 1906. Additionally, Ultsch added a sidewalk to the property and began hosting
moving picture nights at the hotel every Wednesday beginning in 1911.

The Wantagh Hotel circa 1900 (Courtesy of NY Heritage and the Wantagh Preservation Society).

After Ultsch died in 1920, Leo Wetter, and business partner Joseph Sens, bought the hotel around 1925 (""Wantagh Hotel, Early 1900s"). When the business partnership dissolved in 1942, Wetter continued to run the hotel until his sons, Frank and Hans Natter took over in 1947 ("Wantagh Hotel, 1930"). The hotel restaurant served German food and one could get a full meal for around two dollars. The beauty of the Wantagh Hotel came to a tragic end on December 19, 1970, when a fire destroyed the building. The building was then knocked down and replaced by McDonald's.

Chapter Nine: WWI and Jones Beach

Lufberry Field

The first World War once again shattered the farming-centric town of Wantagh. The United States officially declared war in 1917, and after this declaration, two small airfields sanctioned by the US army were constructed on Long Island. One of these airfields was located in Wantagh and was known as Lufberry Field. The field was known as such to honor aviation ace Raoul Lufberry. Lufberry had flown for both the French and American air services and was killed during a combat mission in May of 1918. The field itself was "located south of Merrick Road and east of Wantagh Parkway," according to Jim Colotti, the newsletter editor for the Wantagh Preservation Society. Those who were stationed at the field, between 200 to 400 men in total, lived in barracks that were north of Merrick Road. Nearby proximity to water allowed for a prime sport to practice flying, with the base having twelve Curtiss JN-4 airplanes assigned to it. Most American pilots during the war trained with one of these planes, nicknamed "The Jenny"("Wantagh Military Air Base").

The barracks at Lufberry Field (Courtesy of NY Heritage and the Wantagh Preservation Society).

Many brave Wantagh residents fought in the Great War. One of these individuals was Leroy T. Wells. Wells, born in Wantagh in 1893, served in WWI in France with the Rainbow Division in 1917.

According to Eric Durr, the Director of Public Affairs at the New York State Division of Military and Naval Affairs, the Rainbow Division was composed of National Guard units from across the country combined into one unit. This was done to prevent any region or state in the U.S. from becoming angry if one state division was sent to France first instead of them. The division was called the Rainbow Division, as General McArthur Douglas stated the division would stretch out across the United States "like a rainbow"(Durr).

Wells was wounded in action in October of 1918. He held a Croix de Guerre, or "War Cross," which was a French military decoration used to honor acts of bravery during both world wars. After the war, Leroy Wells continued to remain active in the community. According to the Wantagh Preservation Society, he "was a member of the Disabled Officers Association and the Wantagh American Legion Post No. 1273... the Wantagh Mutual Association and was a member of the Wantagh Fire Department from 1912-1942" ("Leroy T. Wells").

Leroy T. Wells (Courtesy of NY Heritage and the Wantagh Preservation Society).

While many Wantagh individuals returned home safely from the war, one man did not. Bergen R. Seaman was the only Wantagh man to die during the war. Seaman's childhood home still stands near the St. Markella Greek Orthodox Church. A gold star can be seen next to Bergen Seaman's name on the memorial, honoring him as a man who sacrificed his life for his country.

The war ended in November of 1918. A memorial commemorating Wantagh residents who fought in the war was dedicated in 1919. The original memorial was taken down years ago, but a new memorial was built in its exact location on Railroad Avenue in 2018.

The original WWI memorial on Railroad Avenue, date unknown (Courtesy of NY Heritage and the Wantagh Preservation Society).

The new WWI memorial.

Jones Beach

After WWI, many Americans needed a place to relax. Jones Beach between the two world wars became this place for numerous Americans.

The story of Jones Beach began in the early 1920s with a man named Robert Moses. Robert Moses, born in 1888, changed the physical landscape of New York state forever. In 1924, New York Governor Alfred E. Smith appointed Moses as the head of both the New York and Long Island state parks commissions. This position allowed Moses to work on, and be in charge of, numerous public projects, including the construction of the Queens Midtown Tunnel and the Triborough Bridge.

Early on in his career, which lasted decades, Moses had the idea for the construction of Jones Beach State Park. It was 1926, and he had the vision to create a meandering parkway that would eventually give one access to the beach and the Atlantic Ocean. He decided to utilize the now-dormant lands that had once been a part of the Ridgewood Aqueduct. After claiming these lands that same year, Moses set to work building the parkway and reforming Jones Beach into an ideal summer getaway location. After changing the physical landscape of the beach, as previously the beach was underwater at high tide, his dream of creating a beautiful parkway, and a beach to go along with it, became a reality ("Robert Moses").

Jones Beach officially opened to the public in 1929. The beach, among other buildings, contained two bathhouses and a water tower, more commonly referred to by local residents as the Jones Beach Needle or Pencil, that would be a focal point of the beach. New York City residents flocked to the area to escape the sounds and sights of city life. Because of the destination's popularity, Wantagh has been aptly nicknamed "the gateway to Jones Beach."

Jones Beach Watertower, circa 1950 (Courtesy of NY Heritage and the Wantagh Preservation Society).

While Robert Moses was incredibly influential in molding Wantagh into what it is today, it is important to note that Moses, in constructing his projects, often did so to the annoyance of the communities nearby. According to some records, Moses had forced thousands of residents to leave their homes so that he could construct some of his projects. Thus it must be said that while Moses has done much for the Wantagh community, one must think of the negative aspects of the man and his projects as well.

Chapter Ten: The Brush and St.Matthias Church

The Brush was a thriving community originally composed of previously enslaved individuals who were freed both immediately after the American Revolution and later on, such as with a man named George Lawrence.

George Lawrence and his wife were freed from bondage by local Quakers around 1830. After gaining freedom, Lawrence and his wife built a house on Old Mill Road, today known as the Lawrence House. The Lawrence family owned the home for three generations until 1934. The family would farm the land that they had, and were quite successful in their endeavors. The house, which was considered to be a part of the Brush, was later owned by the Farrell Family ("Lawrence House, 1880 Old Mill Rd.").

The Lawrence House on Old Mill Road was built in 1830 (Courtesy of NY Heritage and the Wantagh Preservation Society).

The Lawrence House today.

While the Brush itself began somewhat after the American Revolution, the community really began to take shape in the mid-nineteenth century. The community was also composed of individuals of Native American descent. As previously stated, The Brush would have been located in western Wantagh, around where Oakfield Avenue is today, and would have stretched into present-day Bellmore. The Brush was likely named as such due to the area being heavily wooded, with pine and scrub oak throughout (Mackey).

Children sitting on a bridge near the entrance to the Brush on Beltagh Avenue, today near the middle and high school (Courtesy of NY Heritage and the Wantagh Preservation Society).

According to Gary Hammond, a former Trustee of the Wantagh Preservation Society, a school was built for Black children in the area by the Quakers as early as 1835. This was the earliest attempt to help Black residents of Wantagh, Jerusalem at this time, in terms of education (Hammond).

The Brush remained a thriving community for hundreds of years. In the early 20th century, there was a significant amount of Black families living in the area. After the second world war, these numbers significantly dropped and today, the majority of Wantagh is white. This racial demographic shift may be attributed to the idea of suburbia that developed after WWII. After the war, many white families moved to the suburbs of Long Island, specifically in Levittown, and settled down. It is possible that this influx of white individuals is the cause of the Black community living in Wantagh to steadily decrease.

St.Matthias Church

One building that was central to life in the Brush was the Saint Matthias Church. The church, which can still be seen today on Jerusalem Avenue, was built in 1904 after the original church building, which was located on Oakfield Avenue, was destroyed in a fire in the late nineteenth century. The original church, known as the African Methodist Episcopal (AME) Zion Church, was built in the 1830s, and by 1845, had about forty-seven members, and was the hub of religious and social activity for the Brush.

The site of the original church is where the landmarked "Old Burying Grounds" is, more properly known as the St. Matthias Church Cemetery. In this cemetery, about 108 members of the church are laid to rest. The cemetery was an active burial site until 1943. Five Black Union Army Civil War veterans are buried at the site. The cemetery is also the final resting place for descendants of enslaved individuals, according to records from the 1860s. There are only four headstones that remain in the cemetery. (Al-Muslim). The cemetery is often incorrectly referred to by Wantagh residents as "the Indian burial ground."

The St. Matthias Church Cemetery on Oakfield Avenue.

After the 1890s church fire, the congregation became known as the St. Matthias Episcopal Church after the new church was erected on Jerusalem Avenue in 1904. The church was built with money donated by residents of Wantagh, with a majority of these donors being white. The church is incredibly important to Wantagh, and Long Island, history because it is one of the only surviving buildings from the first attempts of the Episcopal Diocese to include non-white individuals from Queens and Nassau Counties in the church. The building is also the second oldest surviving African American religious structure in Nassau County (Hammond). Many of the original features of the church are still intact, including the cornerstone which states the year the church was built, 1904, and the bell tower on the roof of the church. St. Matthias Church received landmark status in 2019.

The St. Matthias Church today. The church is currently closed for the foreseeable future to parishioners.

Chapter Eleven: Wantagh Schools

The very first school in Wantagh today is still in existence, although it sits in Levittown, across the street from MacArthur High School. This school, known as the Jerusalem School, was built in 1876 after it was realized that the children of Jerusalem farmers should receive an education. The school was built on farming land owned by John Birdsall Garner ("Wantagh School Collection").

The schoolhouse was composed of one room. Later on, two additional rooms were added to the structure. Today, the building is recognized as a historic landmark and the building itself currently hosts a private Pre-K facility.

The Jerusalem School building, now a Pre-K facility.

A second schoolhouse was built in 1904. This building built on Beech Street, originally known as Seymour Avenue, was used for teaching elementary students in Wantagh. The school was only four miles away from the original Jerusalem schoolhouse. A few years after the school was built, in 1909, the building was replaced by a larger one and was used as an Elementary school until 1958. This school was the only elementary school in Wantagh until another school was built around 1930. After that, it was used as a school district administration office until 1982. Today, the building is used by a nursery and day camp for Pre-K children ("Wantagh School Collection").

The Seymour Avenue School (Courtesy of NY Heritage and the Wantagh Preservation Society).

The nursery and Pre-K where the Seymour Avenue School was once located.

In 1928, the community approved about $ 230,000.00 in bonds to be used to build another school for the district. This school, called the Sunrise Park School, was built at the corner of Walters Avenue and Cypress Street. The school had eight rooms and was used as an elementary school for decades. In 1989, the school was demolished due to the school's shrinking population and was replaced by houses ("Wantagh School Collection"). Some Wantagh residents remember attending the school before it was shut down.

Sunrise Park School (Courtesy of NY Heritage and the Wantagh Preservation Society).

The housing boom after the Second World War greatly impacted education in Wantagh. The student population of the town increased greatly from 1949 to 1950, with the number of students going from 860 to 1,334, according to the Wantagh Preservation Society. The Society also states that they had to use "a split session schedule due to overcrowding." A new 14-classroom elementary school was built in 1950 on farmland by the Boos' family. This school, incidentally also on Beech St., was used for kindergarten classes and grades two through five. The school today is known as Wantagh Elementary School.

Wantagh Elementary School, circa 1965 (Courtesy of NY Heritage and the Wantagh Preservation Society).

First-grade students took classes at the Seymour Avenue school. Older students, such as those in grades six through eight, went to the Sunrise Park School. And yet, the student population of the town continued to outgrow the schools currently in existence. That is why in 1952, Wantagh residents approved the decision to add twenty-one rooms to the Wantagh School on Beech Street, and twelve more rooms to the Sunrise Park School. In addition to this, Wantagh residents also approved buying land on Beltagh Avenue for a High School, with a budget of three million dollars to build it.

In 1955, construction was finished on Wantagh High School, which resulted in the student grade levels being rearranged temporarily. This same year, other plots of land were bought to build other schools. This is where Forest Lake Elementary and Mandalay Elementary are today. These elementary schools were completed by the end of the decade. A junior high school, now known as Wantagh Middle School, was completed in 1965 ("Wantagh School Collection").

Wantagh High School, specifically, had many interesting clubs in its early years, including a rifle club and a stamp collecting club.

Wantagh High School circa 1965 (Courtesy of NY Heritage and the Wantagh Preservation Society).

Chapter Twelve: Late 20th Century to Today

<u>Paradise After WWII</u>

After the opening of Jones Beach in 1929, the next major thing to happen to our small farming community was the beginning of World War II. The Second World War began in 1939, with the United States joining the war in 1941. Many Wantagh residents took up the call to fight in the war. The five men who died in the war are remembered with a plaque located at Wantagh High School. These men were Eugene Bradshaw, Henry C. Wagner, James T. Finch, Edward R. Segelken, and Richard A. Van Tuyl. Mr. Van Tuyl's childhood home, located on Elm Place, is landmarked. The house was built by his father, who was an early founder of a Wantagh lumber yard, which later became Nassau Suffolk lumber.

Plaque located in Wantagh High School remembering the men who died in both WWI and WWII.

When the war ended in 1945, many war veterans returned to Wantagh, and Long Island looking for a place to live. This is where the idea of suburbia began. It is around this time that William Levitt, of Levitt & Sons, began to mass-produce identical, and affordable, houses for veterans returning from the war. His first community of houses opened in 1947 and was known as Island Tree, which is now known as Levittown (Cusanelli). This area was perfect for individuals looking to start a family, and many people flocked to Levittown. Originally the town itself was entirely segregated, as Levitt's town had a clause in its covenant that stated they could not sell homes to people of color. This was eventually overturned in a 1948 court case, however, the town still remains mainly white to this day.

The idea of suburbia, or a place to live just outside of a city, was created during this time. Prior to this, many people lived in cities or rural areas. This idea of suburbia eventually came into Wantagh, whether it be for good or bad. In Wantagh, there was an immense need for housing, and a construction explosion began in the area. Because of this, the last of the farms in Wantagh disappeared as farmers sold their lands off to housing developers. The original heart and soul of the settlement of Jerusalem, farming, was now gone forever. In its place, many new houses, although not identical, as was the case with Levittown, were built ("Wantagh Local History").

The Wantagh Library

The Wantagh Public Library was established in February of 1962, after a vote by community members. Originally, the library was located in a small rented space on Park Avenue and opened to the public in December of 1962. It held a collection of 3,000 volumes, three staff members, and numerous volunteers from the community to keep the library running. Some of these volunteers were members of the Friends of the Wantagh Library, a group that was instrumental in establishing the library in the first place.

In 1967, the community approved a bond issue of $495,000 to purchase a plot of land on Park Avenue for the library's permanent location, and to build the library there. The building itself was designed by Henry J. Stojowski, an architect from Lattingtown, Long Island. The building, which is 16,000 square feet and contains a unique center core split-level, was finished and opened to the public in December of 1970. In 1988, the administrative area of the library was expanded ("Wantagh Public Library").

Today, the Wantagh Public Library greatly supports the Wantagh community with both educational resources and recreational events the library hosts. The library currently hosts numerous events including yoga classes, writing classes for students, and music events for families. Wantagh residents can also utilize the library's museum passes for fun educational excursions at various locations.

<u>The Wantagh Museum and the Wantagh Preservation Society</u>

In 1965, the tracks of the Wantagh line of the LIRR were set to be raised due to safety concerns. The original railroad station, from 1885, was set to be demolished. Concerned residents stepped in and decided to save the building. They moved the building from its original home on Railroad Avenue to its current location on Wantagh Avenue. This concerned group of residents formed the Wantagh Preservation Society. The Wantagh Preservation Society runs the Wantagh museum. In 1972, the Jamaica train car was donated to the museum by the Long Island Railroad. The train was a parlor car and contained a lounge area and three staterooms, or sleeping quarters (Hackmack). Today, the Wantagh Preservation Society works to preserve historical sites in Wantagh and to engage the local community with Wantagh's history.

The Wantagh Museum today.

The Jamaica train car today.

Wantagh Today

Today, Wantagh has a population of about 18,000 people. There are currently three elementary schools, one middle school, and one high school. Wantagh residents enjoy their proximity to the beach and New York City. Most residents today are commuters who live in Wantagh but work in Manhattan. Many students enjoy going to Jones Beach frequently and also spend time in neighboring towns such as Bellmore going to the movie theater.

Chapter Thirteen: The People of Wantagh

Wantagh wouldn't be Wantagh without the people in. Every single resident, from its beginnings to today, has contributed to the rich history of this community. Mentioned below are just a fraction of the individuals who have called Wantagh home over the years.

<u>A Historian and Artist</u>

We all owe Margaret Aiken a great deal of thanks for keeping Wantagh's history alive. Aiken was the founder of the Wantagh Preservation Society and led the small group of citizens that ultimately saved the original railroad station from destruction. This group, nicknamed "Margy and her Steamrollers," would become the foundation for the Preservation Society (Mansmann).

In addition to saving Wantagh's history, Margaret Aiken was an artist. Originally from Arizona, she studied art at Arizona State University and Carnegie Institute of Technology. After moving to New York, she worked in Manhattan as a commercial art and fashion illustrator. Aiken is also responsible for the illustrations in *Wantagh Past and Present*, a textbook meant to supplement the curriculum of the middle school in the 1960s. The textbook is no longer in circulation ("Aiken, Margaret").

Photograph of Margaret Aiken. (Courtesy of NYHeritage and the Wantagh Preservation Society).

A Blacksmith and Fire Chief

George E. Box was born in 1863 and held numerous jobs throughout his life in Wantagh. Box was the town's blacksmith who later became the janitor for the Seymour Avenue School. It is within his blacksmith shop that he built Wantagh's first fire pump in 1910. Box was a member of the Wantagh Fire Department for decades and in 1905, he served as chief of the department. He served as chief again from 1910 to 1914 and was a member of the fire department from 1900 up until his death in 1943. George was also a member of the Wantagh Mutual Assistance Association and served as its president from 1904 to 1905 and from 1911 to 1912. In addition, he was also a member of the Board of Education ("George E. Box").

Photograph of George E. Box (Courtesy of NYHeritage and the Wantagh Preservation Society).

In 1900, George married Maria Seaman a year after his first wife died. Maria Box, nee Seaman, was an active member of the Wantagh Congregational Church. Before she married Box, Maria worked in a fly net factory owned by the Lee Brothers. She later worked as a dressmaker. After marriage, she became a stepmother to Box's five daughters, who were known locally as "the Box Sisters." Maria passed away in 1942 at the age of 76 ("Maria Seaman Box").

Photograph of Maria Box, nee Seaman (Courtesy of NYHeritage and the Wantagh Preservation Society).

A Man on the Moon

David Steen is one of the few individuals on this Earth who has their name permanently on the moon. Steen was an electrical engineer for Grumman's space program. He was in charge of designing the device that would ultimately cut the link between the part of the lunar module that the astronauts were using to travel home, and the part that would be left behind on the moon. Steen was described as being incredibly devoted and proud of the work he was doing while at Grumman's, as well as his other work with a defense company.

David Steen was born in Queens in 1923. At the age of 19, he volunteered for the Navy at the outbreak of WWII. During the war, he learned how to repair airplane radios damaged in combat. After the war, he attended Brooklyn Polytechnic and became an electrical engineer. In 1952, he married Jean Ferris and the two later moved to Wantagh. It is around this time that Grumman recruited Steen for the job of supervising the design and construction of the device that cut the link between two parts of the shuttle.

Steen's name is on the Lunar Excursion Module that was left on the moon after the moon landing. His name is alongside the names of the three astronauts who landed on the moon, as well as everyone else involved in the moon landing (Holm).

The People of Wantagh

Mrs. Hunt and Miss Alice Southerland, founders of the Good Cheer Club. The Good Cheer Club was a church group with the Wantagh Memorial Congregational Church (Courtesy of NY Heritage and the Wantagh Preservation Society).

Mr. and Mrs. John Cowles standing on Old Mill Road and Beltagh Avenue circa 1897. The two are standing next to the sluiceway, or gate that controls the flow of water into the mill. This would have been taken near where Forest Lake Elementary School stands today. The two lived on Wantagh Avenue and Mr. Cowles was a member of the Wantagh Fire Department and Board of Education. He was also a designer (Courtesy of NY Heritage and the Wantagh Preservation Society).

John Davis sitting in his automobile, one of the first in Wantagh (Courtesy of NY Heritage and the Wantagh Preservation Society).

An outing at Jones Beach (Courtesy of NY Heritage and the Wantagh Preservation Society).

Bibliography

"1885 Ridgewood Station." *New York Heritage*, Wantagh Preservation Society.

"1885 Wantagh Station." *New York Heritage*, Wantagh Preservation Society.

"About Long Island New York." *LongIsland.com*.

"Aiken, Margaret." *New York Heritage*, Wantagh Preservation Society.

Al-Muslim, Aisha. "Town Weighs Landmark Status for African-American Cemetery in Wantagh." *Newsday*, Newsday, 18 Apr. 2014.

"Animism." *Encyclopædia Britannica*, Encyclopædia Britannica, Inc.

"Battle of Long Island." *Encyclopædia Britannica*, Encyclopædia Britannica, Inc.

"Brooklyn Water Works Construction, Ridgewood Station, 1888." *New York Heritage*, Wantagh Preservation Society.

"Children on Bridge across Wantagh River." *New York Heritage*, Wantagh Preservation Society.

Cummins, Joseph. "Algonquin Beliefs in Spirits & Nature." *The Classroom | Empowering Students in Their College Journey*, 5 Nov. 2021.

Cusanelli, Michael. "Levittown Turns 70 Today: Photos of America's 1st Suburb." *Newsday*, Newsday, 30 Apr. 2019.

Diouf, Sylviane. "New York City's Slave Market." *The New York Public Library*, The New York Public Library, 1 Feb. 2021.

Durr, Eric. *"Rainbow Division" That Represented the United States Formed in New York in August 1917*. U.S. Army, 24 July 2017.

"Elvin Bodley, Wantagh Station Agent." *New York Heritage Digital Collections*, Wantagh Preservation Society.

Fabricant, Florence. "Pickles by the Barrel." *The New York Times*, 2 Sept. 1979.

Feldmann, Aissa. "Hempstead Plains Grassland." *Hempstead Plains Grassland Guide - New York Natural Heritage Program*, 22 June 2021.

"Fussell Brothers Boarding Stables, Wantagh." *New York Heritage*, Wantagh Preservation Society.

"Fussell's General Store & 1907 Post Office." *New York Heritage*, Wantagh Preservation Society.

"George E. Box." *New York Heritage*, Wantagh Preservation Society.

"Gristmill & Birdsall-Mill House, Early 1900's." *New York Heritage*, Wantagh Preservation Society.

Hackmack, Andrew. "Old Train Car to Get Some TLC." *Long Island Herald*, Herald Community Newspapers, 1 May 2015.

Hammond, Gary. "The Mystery Church." *Wantagh LI*, Wantagh Preservation Society, Apr. 2019.

"Harold Avenue Cemetery." *Hempstead Town, NY*.

"Hempstead Convention of 1665 and Duke's Laws." *Historical Society of the New York Courts*, 24 Jan. 2019.

"Henry Hudson." *History.com*, A&E Television Networks, 9 Nov. 2009.

Holm, Erik. "David Steen, Grumman Space Program Engineer." 2000.

The Information Window. Wantagh Preservation Society, 2012.

"John Davis." *New York Heritage*, Wantagh Preservation Society.

"Lawrence House, 1880 Old Mill Rd." *New York Heritage*, Wantagh Preservation Society.

"Leroy T. Wells." *NY Heritage*, Wantagh Preservation Society.

"Long Island Surnames." *Long Island Surnames*, Long Island Genealogy.

"Long Island." *Long Island | A Tour of New Netherland*, New Netherland Institute.

Mackey, Linda. "St. Matthias Church Resource Evaluation ." *Preservation Long Island*, New York State Office of Parks, Recreation and Historic Preservation, 16 May 2019.

Mansmann, Julie. "Getting a Glimpse of Wantagh's Past." *Herald Community Newspapers*, Herald Community Newspapers, 27 Sept. 2016.

Manton, Paul. "John Seaman: Founding Father." *Levittown, NY Patch*, Patch, 30 Jan. 2013.

"Maria Seaman Box." *New York Heritage*, Wantagh Preservation Society.

Martine, David. "Native American Wigwam." *Sylvester Manor Educational Farm*.

McKernan, Gordon, et al. *Wantagh Past and Present*. Dept. of Curriculum Development, Wantagh Union Free School District, 1975.

Morrison, David D. *Long Island Rail Road: Babylon Branch*. Arcadia Publishing, 2021.

"Mr. & Mrs. John Cowles, Old Mill & Beltagh 1897." *New York Heritage*, Wantagh Preservation Society.

"Mrs. Hunt & Miss Alice Southerland, Founders of Good Cheer Club." *New York Heritage*, Wantagh Preservation Society.

National Geographic Society. "Women and Children in Colonial America." *National Geographic Society*, 19 Feb. 2020.

"New York Slave Rebellion of 1712." *Encyclopædia Britannica*, Encyclopædia Britannica, Inc.

O'Connor-Arena, Melissa. "Benjamin Birdsall Homestead." *Wantagh-Seaford, NY Patch*, Patch, 19 July 2011.

"On This Day: 'No Taxation without Representation!'." *National Constitution Center*.

"Outing at High Hill Pavilion." *New York Heritage*, Wantagh Preservation Society.

"Overview of the American Revolutionary War." *American Battlefield Trust*, 25 Aug. 2021.

"Parmenus Jackson Sr.." *WikiTree*, 8 Jan. 2022.

Pfeiffer, Karl F. *Althouse*. Wantagh American Revolution Bicentennial Committee.

"Phebe Wilmarth Wells." *New York Heritage*, Wantagh Preservation Society.

Prine Pauls, Elizabeth. "Tribe." *Encyclopædia Britannica*, Encyclopædia Britannica, Inc.

"Quaker Meeting House, East Side of Wantagh Ave near Twin Lane." *New York Heritage*, Wantagh Preservation Society.

"Quakers." *History.com*, A&E Television Networks, 19 May 2017.

Rincon, Paul. "Earliest Evidence for Humans in the Americas." *BBC News*, BBC, 22 July 2020.

"Robert Moses." Edited by Kathleen Kuiper, *Encyclopædia Britannica*, Encyclopædia Britannica, Inc.

Scott, Michon. "What's the Coldest Earth's Ever Been?" *What's the Coldest Earth's Ever Been? | NOAA Climate.gov*, 18 Feb. 2021.

Seibel, Vicky. "Denton Rev. Richard." *The Seibel Family Stories*.

Soter, Steven. *Cosmic Horizons: Astronomy at the Cutting Edge*. New Press, 2001.

Strong, John A. *The Algonquian Peoples of Long Island: From Earliest Times to 1700*. Empire State Books, 1997.

Sturtevant, William C. *Handbook of North American Indians*. Vol. 15, Smithsonian Institution, 1978.

"Sunrise Park School." *New York Heritage*, Wantagh Preservation Society.

"Theodore J. Wells." *New York Heritage*, Wantagh Preservation Society.

Toscano, C. *Jackson-Jones Family Collection, 1685-1865*. Hofstra University, 8 Oct. 2015.

"The Tribes of Long Island." *On This Site*, 27 May 2020.

Villani, Robert. *Long Island: A Natural History*. Abrams, 1997, pp. 9-13.

"Wantagh Ave Looking South to Merrick Rd." *New York Heritage*, Wantagh Preservation Society.

"Wantagh Fire Department." *New York Heritage*, Wantagh Preservation Society.

"Wantagh Fire Dept.- Sam Myers Truck - Hook & Ladder Co. 1." *New York Heritage*, Wantagh Preservation Society.

"Wantagh Fire Station No. 1, 1910." *New York Heritage*, Wantagh Preservation Society.

"Wantagh High School, Oct 1965." *New York Heritage*, Wantagh Preservation Society.

"Wantagh Hotel, 1930." *New York Heritage*, Wantagh Preservation Society.

"Wantagh Hotel, Early 1900's." *New York Heritage*, Wantagh Preservation Society.

"Wantagh Local History." *Wantagh Local History | New York Heritage*.

"Wantagh Memorial Congregational Church." *New York Heritage*, Wantagh Preservation Society.

Wantagh Military Air Base. Edited by Jim Colotti, Wantagh Preservation Society.

"Wantagh Post Office, Park Avenue, Oct. 1965." *New York Heritage*, Wantagh Preservation Society.

"Wantagh Public Library." *New York Heritage*, Wantagh Preservation Society.

"Wantagh School Collection." *New York Heritage*, Wantagh Preservation Society.

"Wantagh's First Schoolhouse." *New York Heritage*, Wantagh Preservation Society.

"War of 1812." *History.com*, A&E Television Networks, 27 Oct. 2009.

Watson, Tom. "Letter to Editor: Clearing up Confusion on Two Jackson Cemeteries." *Wantagh-Seaford, NY Patch*, Patch, 27 July 2011.

"When Did Slavery End in New York State?" *New York Historical Society*.

"Whitmore, Emma, Wantagh Station Agent." Wantagh Preservation Society.

Wiebel, Ted. "Quaker Meeting House." *New York Heritage*.

Wolley, Charles. *A Two Years Journal in New York: And Part of Its Territories in America*. The Burrows Brothers Company, 1902.

Wood, Silas. *A Sketch of the First Settlement of the Several Towns on Long Island*. A. Spooner, 1828.

Yost, Russell. "Adriaen Block Facts, Voyages, and Accomplishments - the ..." *The History Junkie*.

Acknowledgments

This novel would not have been possible without the immense support I received from the Wantagh Preservation Society. A huge thank you to Tom Watson for spending time helping me fact-check my information and proofreading the novel. Thank you for believing in me and what I wished to accomplish.

Thank you a.so to the rest of the preservation society for also taking the time to edit this piece, with a special thank you to members Carol Poulos and Pete McHale for all of their help.

This novel also would not have been possible without the support of Anna Lenz, my Girl Scout Gold Award mentor. From answering my frantic emails to proofreading my work, she did it all. Thank you for providing guidance and support when I needed it most.

To my Girl Scout troop leaders Lynn Morris and Jean Blom, your support throughout the years means the world to me. Thank you for encouraging me to go for my Gold.

To the community members, family, and friends who cheered me on throughout this process, thank you for believing in me. I hope you learned something along the way!

Finally, thank you to my parents. You have been my biggest supporters throughout this entire process, and I couldn't have done it without you. From the bottom of my heart, thank you.

About the Author

Emma Alexander is a recent graduate of Wantagh High School. This book was a part of her Girl Scout Gold Award project, the highest award in Girl Scouting. Emma has a passion for history and the language arts. She is looking forward to her next chapter at Cornell University starting in the fall of 2022.

Made in the USA
Coppell, TX
02 April 2023